CANALS & RIVERS:
YESTERDAY & TODAY

Anthony T. Brown

Foreword by
Timothy West CBE

Country Books

Published by Country Books/Ashridge Press
Courtyard Cottage, Little Longstone, Bakewell, Derbyshire DE45 1NN

Tel: 01629 640670
e-mail: dickrichardson@country-books.co.uk
www.countrybooks.biz

ISBN 978-1-906789-25-1

Printed and bound in England by 4edge Ltd, Hockley, Essex

DEDICATION

This book is dedicated, with love and appreciation to my lifetime companion and soul mate, my wife Beryl Kay.

FOREWORD

Dr Anthony Brown, a keen devotee and user of our Inland Waterways, has over the years collected a fascinating archive of engravings celebrating not only the rural beauty peculiar to waterside landscape, but also the achievement of the architects, bridge-builders and canal engineers of the Industrial Revolution.

Facing each engraving is a present-day photograph of the same site. In many cases, capturing the scene from the exact same viewpoint has proved impossible due to the growth of abundant foliage, but this should not be taken to indicate that the author/photographer is unwilling to go out in the winter: the pictures serve quite well enough to identify the location, and point more clearly to the salient points of change.

Some of these changes, though necessary, are rather depressing. The fine 1754 Old Bridge in Bath has been replaced by a featureless span of concrete and to carry the River Irwell over the Manchester Ship Canal, James Brindley's stone construction had to give way to an ingenious but unattractive metal swing aqueduct. On the other hand, the nearby City Basin is a fine example of the intelligent canalside restoration and development that is thankfully going on in the area.

Occasionally, comparing the pairs of images, it is surprising how little change has taken place. On the Thames, at least at Richmond and above, very little seems to have been allowed to encroach on the green spaces, hedgerows, locks and weirs, houses and churches that appear in the engravings. However the Regent's Canal, well-served in the collection, has certainly changed over the years. In the 1820s and 30s the 'Paddington Packet', with its load of day-trippers, had to thread its way between a cavelcade of commercial barges; today it is a mooring-place for privately-owned narrowboats. Every picture, as they say, tells a story.

The engraver is generally out to capture the pastoral beauty of rivers, while his attitude to man-made canals tends to be more pragmatic and respectful. But in the picture (cl840) of the astonishing Pontcysyllte Aqueduct, with the River Dee below, we get both. The photograph opposite, taken to include the weir and with the added bonus of a narrowboat and a few fearless pedestrians, achieves the same effect. It's a sublime marriage of art with nature.

Timothy West CBE
2011

PREFACE

The idea for this book arose during a canal trip on my narrowboat 'Cantabile' whilst visiting the town of Congleton in Cheshire. A browse in a small antique shop there revealed a small but interesting engraving of the Pontcysyllte Aquaduct which carries the Llangollen Canal over the River Dee Valley in North Wales and which graces the front cover of this book. This was the start of a collection of over fifty engravings of canal and river scenes, dating from 1770 to 1890, most of which are reproduced, with their modern appearances, in this book. The engraving title in larger font and inverted commas reproduces the title on the print and is followed by additional location information where necessary. Where known, the names of the artist followed by the engraver are provided.

Capturing today's images has been something of a challenge. Identifying the exact location was occasionally a problem in spite of extensive research and help from more experts than I could mention. No doubt readers will let us know of any failures in this area!

Sometimes the title of the original engraving was less than helpful and often many of the original features – in some cases, even the waterway – were missing. Usually, artistic licence has enabled the artist to enhance and approximate aesthetic features to bring them together in the same scene, whilst diminishing less attractive items. Frequently the erection of buildings and the growth of trees and foliage made the original viewpoint impractical and frequent compromise in the taking of photographs was required.

The object of this series is to revisit some infrequently seen and often very picturesque engravings and I make no claim to artistic merit in the accompanying photographs which are provided merely to show how things have or have not changed over the last couple of hundred years.

Anthony T. Brown
Nunthorpe, 2011

ACKNOWLEDGEMENTS

My thanks are due to all the archivists and librarians involved with the buildings and structures which appear in the engravings and who have generously given their time and advice to provide the necessary background information to accompany the images. In many cases, passers-by and local residents have been a good source of advice, particularly in the most likely location of photographic vantage points. A special thanks to the gentleman who invited me to photograph the Thames from the balcony of his up-market, high-level, riverside flat.

Mr. Ian Graham of Wilderness Boats who gave me so much advice and encouragement during my early canal boating days, to fit out one of his trailboat shells which initiated my interest in the waterways system both here and in France.

My cousin and fellow narrowboater Tricia Luckcuck who generously offered to proof read and comment on the draft.

Finally, to my wife Beryl, who as usual has shown both support and tolerance in helping to see this project to a conclusion.

These engravings and photographs have been published on a monthly basis in *Canals Rivers and Boats* since November 2010.

Private publication
ISBN 978-1-906789-23-7
Private publication

By the same author:

Kyloe to Cleveland – 300 years of Northumbrian Family History
Tom Brown, Victorian Middlesbrough Dentist
The Adventures of Max and Mabel

CONTENTS

Part 3: CENTRAL LONDON

15 'ENTRANCE TO THE REGENT'S CANAL, LIMEHOUSE'

16 'PARK VILLAGE EAST, REGENT'S PARK'

17 'PADDINGTON CANAL' Tollhouse

18 'JUNCTION OF THE REGENT'S CANAL, AT PADDINGTON' Little Venice I

19 'THE PADDINGTON CANAL' Little Venice II

20 'LONDON, FROM THE TOWER OF ST. SAVIOUR'S CHURCH'

21 'ON THE THAMES AT LOW WATER' Blackfriars

22 'NEW IRON BRIDGE, OVER THE THAMES FROM QUEEN STREET' Southwark

23 'WESTMINSTER, SHOWING THE ABBEY, HALL, BRIDGE ETC.'

24 'SOMERSET HOUSE, LONDON'

25 'BATTERSEA'

26 'FULHAM CHURCH, FROM THE THAMES'

27 'SUSPENSION BRIDGE, OVER THE THAMES AT HAMMERSMITH'

28 'THE DOUBLE LOCK AND EAST ENTRANCE TO THE ISLINGTON TUNNEL, REGENT'S CANAL'

29 'TUNNEL, REGENT'S CANAL' Islington

30 'CITY BASIN, REGENT'S CANAL'

31 'MACCLESFIELD BRIDGE, REGENT'S PARK'

Part 4: OUTER LONDON

32 'GREENWICH HOSPITAL'

33 'ISLEWORTH'

34 'TWICKENHAM, MIDDLESEX'

35 'RICHMOND'

36 'KINGSTON BRIDGE' Kingston upon Thames

37 'THE THAMES AT COWAY STAKES' Walton on Thames

38 'SUNBURY LOCKS' Sunbury on Thames, Surrey

39 'STAINES BRIDGE' Staines, Surrey

40 'KEW BRIDGE, FROM THE FERRY AT BRENTFORD' Kew

Part 5: SOUTH OF ENGLAND

41 'BEAUMONT LODGE, NEAR OLD WINDSOR'   Berkshire

42 'DORNEY CHURCH, BUCKS'   Boveney, Buckinghamshire

43 'A VIEW OF CLIEFDEN (sic) HOUSE FROM MAIDENHEAD BRIDGE'
   Maidenhead, Berkshire

44 'HEDSOR' Buckinghamshire

45 'HARLEYFORD HOUSE' Marlow, Buckinghamshire

46 'WALLINGFORD, BERKSHIRE' Now in Oxfordshire

47 'OSNEY LOCK' Oxford

48 'ENTRANCE TO THE TUNNEL, LEADING TO SAPPERTON HILL,
   GLOUCESTERSHIRE'

49 'AQUEDUCT OF THE KENNET AND AVON CANAL AT LIMPLEY STOKE,
   NEAR BATH'

50 'THE OLD BRIDGE, BATH'

1 'THE CALEDONIAN CANAL'
TOMNAHURICH, INVERNESS
1880

Tomnahurich Bridge in this view was designed by Crouch and Hogg in 1937 and carries the A82, Inverness to Fort William road over the Caledonian Canal in the city of Inverness. It was drawn from Tomnahurich Hill (the hill of the fairies) which is a cemetery opened in the 1850s. The thickness of tree cover which now exists on the hill made it impossible to replicate the engraving artist's exact view so the photograph was taken on the canal towpath, beneath the hill.

2 'BASIN OF THE CALEDONIAN CANAL AT MUIRTOWN NEAR INVERNESS'

1820

S. L. Duff / J. Swaine

This view of the Muirtown Basin on the Caledonian Canal in Inverness is taken from the British Waterways office and shows in the distance, the Muirtown Locks Swing Bridge which carries the A862, Inverness to Beauly Road. Plannned by Thomas Telford, the Caledonian Canal runs for 60 miles along the Great Glen from Corpach near Fort William in the West to Inverness in the East and was completed by 1822. It enables boats to sail from the East to the West coast of Scotland without having to brave the wild seas of the Pentland Firth between the North of Scotland and the Orkney Isles.

3 'BERWICK FROM THE SOUTH EAST'
BERWICK-UPON-TWEED

c.1840

G. Baliner / W. Finden

Berwick upon Tweed is the most northerly town in England and is situated on the northern bank and near the mouth of the River Tweed in Northumberland. This engraving shows the old red sandstone bridge dating from 1611. In the photograph the two other bridges behind it can also be seen. These are the Royal Tweed Bridge, a road bridge built in 1925 to carry the A1, and the Royal Border Bridge, an impressive railway viaduct opened by Queen Victoria in 1850 which still carries the East Coast main line from London to Edinburgh. At the time of the engraving, Berwick was a very busy port both in the fishing and manufacturing industries.

4 'OUSE BRIDGE, YORK'

1784

I. Peake

Published by S. Hooper

Following the collapse of the medieval Ouse Bridge during a flood in 1564, the replacement bridge above was completed in 1566 with 5 arches, the central one 81 feet wide and 17 feet high. Daniel Defoe described it in 1724 as the greatest in England. It was demolished in 1810 and replaced by the current bridge after 10 year's construction.

5 'SELBY BRIDGE'
SELBY, YORKSHIRE
c.1834
N. Whittock / W. J. Cooke
Published by I. T. Hinton

The current Selby Swing Bridge has been standing since 1970, becoming toll-free in 1991 and it replaced the earlier structure which dates back to 1791. It crosses the River Ouse which runs from Linton-on-Ouse in the north where the River Ure and Ripon Canal carry the navigation to Ripon and south to Goole where it meets the river Humber.

Selby Abbey can still be seen in the background, standing here grandly, as it has for almost 1,000 years.

6 'VIEW OF THE DUKE OF BRIDGEWATER'S AQUEDUCT OVER THE RIVER MERSEY'
BARTON-UPON-IRWELL, ECCLES, GREATER MANCHESTER
1766
Published by the Gentleman's Magazine

The Bridgewater Canal carried over the River Irwell on Brindley's 1761 stone aqueduct was built by the Duke of Bridgewater to transport coal more economically from his mines at Worsley to feed Manchester's industrial revolution. However, the construction of the Manchester Ship Canal to give the city direct access to the sea required the stone aqueduct to be replaced by the 1893 Barton Swing Aqueduct to allow clearance for ships to pass on the new canal beneath. The Swing Aqueduct has a steel trough carrying 1,500 tons of water enclosed by gates at both ends and it pivots on an island in the Ship Canal.

7 'AQUEDUCT ON THE PEAK FOREST CANAL
OVER THE RIVER MERSEY'
MARPLE, STOCKPORT
1814

Craig / H. R. Cook
Published by R. Wilks

One of the wonders of the Cheshire Ring, the three-arch, 309 feet long Marple Aqueduct carries the Peak Forest Canal over the River Goyt, 9 miles south east of Manchester. Begun in 1794, building took seven years and cost seven men their lives. Having fallen into disrepair in the 1960s, it has now been restored and made a listed structure. The aqueduct, seen in the engraving from the valley side, is now too surrounded by trees to be easily visible from this point, so the photograph was taken from the tow path of the aqueduct itself.

8 'LIVERPOOL'

1837

S. Davenport
Published by Thomas Kelly

This engraving of Liverpool waterfront from across the River Mersey in Birkenhead looks very different today. The sailing ships have been replaced by the Liverpool to Birkenhead ferry and prominent on today's waterfront are the Liver Building with its two towers and to its right, the Port of Liverpool Building in the centre of the photograph. The very modern, white sloped building to its right is the new Museum of Liverpool which is the largest newly-built national museum in the UK for over a hundred years.

9 'PONTCYSYLTTE AQUEDUCT IN THE VALE OF LLANGOLLEN, DENBIGHSHIRE'

LLANGOLLEN, WALES

c. 1840

This magnificent structure, the longest and highest aqueduct in Britain carries the Llangollen Canal over the Dee Valley in North Wales. It is a Grade I Listed structure and in 2009 became a World Heritage Site. It was built by Thomas Telford and William Jessop between 1795 and 1805 and consists of a cast iron trough carried on nineteen masonry pillars. The aqueduct measures 1,007 feet in length, is 125 feet in height and can be crossed by boat or on foot. The photograph was taken from the pack horse bridge seen in the foreground of the engraving.

10 'BURSTING OF THE NAPTON
AND WARWICK CANAL'
WARWICK
1869
Published by the Illustrated London News

This engraving shows the canal burst near Emscote Bridge where the canal crosses the River Avon. A rowing boat can be seen being swept down the hill towards the railway embankment, watched by a crowd of onlookers on the far bank, right hand side. This location is now part of the Grand Union Canal, Main Line, on the eastern outskirts of Warwick.

11 'WORCESTER'
1847
T. Creswick / W. Miller

This engraving of Worcester Cathedral, rebuilt in 1084, shows the view from the meadows on the west side of the River Severn. On the left hand side is the slender St. Andrew's Spire, also known as 'Glover's Needle, built in 1751. Trees on the bank now prevent a photograph from this viewpoint so it was taken from Worcester Bridge off to the left of the engraving.

12 'STRATFORD-UPON-AVON, WARWICKSHIRE'

1845

Published by Dugdales

The River Avon has been navigable to Stratford since the early 17th century and is now navigable from Tewkesbury to Alveston, just north east of Stratford with a proposal for an extension to connect it to the Grand Union Canal at Warwick.

Across the River Avon is the 13th century Holy Trinity Parish Church, reputedly the most visited parish church in England on account of the fact that William Shakespeare was baptized here, served as a lay rector of the church, and is buried in the chancel. In the foreground is Colin P. Witter Lock, the former Stratford Lock, rebuilt in 1971 by the men of Gloucester Gaol and other volunteers, using an unusual girder structure because of its depth and the unstable ground conditions.

13 'SHIPMEADOW LOCK, ON THE WAVENEY'
NORFOLK
1878
J. Stark / W. Forrest

The River Waveney Navigation was used to transport goods between the towns of Beccles and Yarmouth. The redundant Shipmeadow (Geldeston) Lock illustrated has been at the head of the navigation since 1934, when the previous, additional 7 mile length to Bungay was closed. The engraving, dated 1878 is taken from an earlier picture and the Geldeston Locks Inn is to the right hand side. This pleasant country pub must be among the least accessible in the country, being reached down a mile or two of rough, unmade road but this is compensated for by the warm welcome visitors will receive!

14 'SCENE ON THE RIVER ORWELL AT IPSWICH, SUFFOLK'

c. 1842

Published by Dugdales

A dock had been in operation in Ipswich on a bend in the River Orwell since the 7th century. The engraving shows Ipswich Docks in the early 19th century from Stoke Bridge.

When the 'Wet Dock' was constructed in 1842, it was 'the biggest enclosed dock in the kingdom' at the time. A major regeneration of the area has taken place since 1999.

15 'ENTRANCE TO THE REGENT'S CANAL, LIMEHOUSE'

LONDON

1828

T. H. Shepherd / E. J. Havell
Published by Jones & Company

Limehouse Basin provides a navigable link between the Regent's Canal and the River Thames, through the Limehouse Basin Lock. The photograph is taken from the south bank of the River Thames looking towards the current (1869) entrance to Limehouse Basin, opened in 1820 as the Regent's Canal Dock. The vertical steel piling behind the stern of the cruise boat represents the position of the original entrance as seen on the engraving.

16 'PARK VILLAGE EAST, REGENT'S PARK'
LONDON
1829
T. H. Shepherd / W. Radcliff

The engraving shows the backs of delightful villas still standing in Park Village East, looking south towards Cumberland Market. The 0·6 mile long Cumberland Arm of the canal that connected Cumberland Basin close to Euston Station to the Regent's Canal is now filled in. The arm closed in 1942 and was infilled with rubble from war-damaged London. The dry canal bed and retaining wall with stone arches is just visible in the foreground of the photograph.

17 'PADDINGTON CANAL'
LONDON
1820

The engraving is of the toll house of the Paddington Arm of the Grand Junction Canal dating from 1801. Foliage has made the view impossible to reproduce but the toll office can just be seen in the photograph at the end of the towpath where it is situated next to Westbourne Terrace Bridge. The local councils paid to have stop gates put in here and at Warwick Avenue and Ladbroke Grove during 1940 because of concerns that any bombs hitting the canal would cause flooding to thousands of homes. Until the late 1980s the toll office was British Waterways' London Head Office and since has been used as commercial offices.

18 'JUNCTION OF THE REGENT'S CANAL,
AT PADDINGTON'
LONDON
1828
T. H. Shepherd / S. Lacey
Published by Jones & Company

Little Venice is the well-known London canal basin at the junction of the Paddington arm of the Grand Union canal and the Regent's Canal and is said to have been named by Robert Browning. This view is from the London Waterbus Company's mooring from which you can take the trip boat on a 50 minute journey through Regent's Park and the zoo to Camden Lock.

19 'THE PADDINGTON CANAL'
LONDON
1840

Another view of Little Venice, this time showing the regular, fast, Paddington Packet Boats loading with rather smartly dressed passengers for the 15 mile trip to Cowley at the junction of the Slough Arm of the Grand Union Canal in Uxbridge, Middlesex. The service began in the early 1800s and ran successfully for a number of years, each boat being pulled by four horses. The public house near the Cowley terminal is still known as the 'Paddington Packet Boat'. The grand, white building in the engraving background can still just be seen today behind the trees on the far side of the canal.

20 'LONDON, FROM THE TOWER OF
ST SAVIOUR'S CHURCH'
1833
Major Yates / S. Davenport
Published by Thomas Kelly

London Bridge, shown here, has a long history but the bridge in the engraving was completed in 1831 and opened by King William IV. It was built of Dartmoor granite and its 5 arches stretched 928 feet from end to end. In 1962, an increase in traffic caused it to start sinking into the Thames so it was auctioned in 1968 and shipped off to Lake Havasu City in the form of numbered blocks where it was reconstructed in 1971. The current bridge was built directly over the old one, without one day's London traffic being lost.

21 'ON THE THAMES AT LOW WATER'
BLACKFRIARS, LONDON
1889

These ragged boys are thought to be 'mudlarks', possibly collecting coal at low tide, with probably the old Blackfriars Bridge or the now demolished railway bridge behind them. They commonly tried to get between the coal barges and knock lumps of coal off into the mud, which they could collect afterwards.

The Society of Thames Mudlarks, founded in 1980, is the modern equivalent and members specialize in searching the Thames mud for treasure and historical artifacts, reporting finds to the Museum of London.

22 'NEW IRON BRIDGE, OVER THE THAMES FROM QUEEN STREET'
SOUTHWARK, LONDON
c. 1819

J. P. Neale / H. Hobson
Published by John Harris, 'Beauties of England and Wales'

Known as the Iron Bridge to distinguish it from the stone London Bridge, Southwark Bridge was designed by John Rennie and opened in 1819. It consisted of three large cast iron spans supported by granite piers and was notable for the central span, at 240 feet (73 m), being the longest cast iron span, ever made.

The 42 feet wide roadway was formed of solid plates of cast iron and supported by stone piers, which rest on timber platforms with wooden pile foundations driven deep into the river bed.

The current, five arch bridge was opened in 1921 by King George V and Queen Mary and given Grade II listed structure status in 1995.

23 'WESTMINSTER, SHOWING THE ABBEY, HALL, BRIDGE, ETC.'

LONDON 1809

W. Anderson / J. Pye
Published by Vernor, Hood & Sharpe, Poultry,
'Beauties of England and Wales'

The engraving shows Labeyle's, stone Westminster Bridge, built 1738 – 1750 with Westminster Abbey in the distance. Owing to subsidence, it was replaced by the current bridge, the oldest bridge in Central London, designed by Thomas Page and built with seven cast iron arches in 1862. Between 2005 and 2007 it was extensively renovated and the decorative cast iron fascia girders were replaced. On the left of the photograph, taken from a slightly different angle, is the Palace of Westminster, also known as the Houses of Parliament, rebuilt following a disastrous fire in 1834.

24 'SOMERSET HOUSE, LONDON'
c.1840
Published Dugdales

Somerset House is a spectacular neo-classical building on the banks of the River Thames in central London, built by Sir William Chambers between 1775 and 1801. Severe damage caused by a direct hit by a bomb in October 1940 was repaired by 1952. It was used from 1837 when civil registration was set up as the office of the Registrar General of Births, Marriages and Deaths, and later for other government purposes. Today, Somerset House is a major arts and culture centre with a year-round programme of open-air concerts, films, large-scale contemporary exhibitions and events.

25 'BATTERSEA'
LONDON
1805
Schnebbelic / Woolnoth
Published by I. Stratford, 'Dr. Hughson's Description of London'

Old Battersea Bridge, shown in the engraving was built in timber in 1772 by architect Henry Holland as a toll bridge to replace the previous Chelsea/Battersea ferry service. At only 24 feet wide it was not a great success aggravated by the frequent repairs required following ships colliding with the many pillars supporting the nineteen spans. The addition of lighting and railings did little to improve matters and it was replaced in 1890 by the present five arch cast iron structure designed by Sir Joseph Bazalgette.

St. Mary's Church, Battersea, as seen in the right of the engraving can still be seen from the riverside but the construction of up-market apartments here has made it impractical to include both church and bridge in the same view today.

26 'FULHAM CHURCH, FROM THE THAMES'
LONDON
Published by Cassells, 'Old and New London'

All Saints' Church, Fulham stands on the North Bank of the River Thames at the end of Putney Bridge and next to Fulham Palace, the former home of the Bishops of London. There has been a church on this site for over 900 years but apart from the 14th century tower the current church designed by Sir Arthur Blomfield, dates from the 1880s. Viewed from the South Bank, it is now largely obscured by trees.

27 'SUSPENSION BRIDGE,
OVER THE THAMES AT HAMMERSMITH'
LONDON
1828
T. H. Shepherd / T. Higham
Published by Jones & Company

This engraving of the first suspension bridge over the River Thames was made shortly after its completion as a toll bridge. It was suspended by chains of wrought iron bars from stone towers and the roadway was constructed from strong timbers covered by granite. In 1887 the Prince of Wales opened the stronger, current bridge designed by Sir Joseph Bazalgette which was built on the same pier foundations.

28 'THE DOUBLE LOCK AND EAST ENTRANCE TO THE ISLINGTON TUNNEL, REGENT'S CANAL'

LONDON

1827

T. H. Shepherd / F. J. Havell
Published by Jones & Company

This is City Road Lock which is situated between the eastern portal of the Islington Tunnel and City Road Basin. As seen in the engraving it is equipped for double working, with two Pickfords' commercial boats leaving one of the locks, but in the photograph the second chamber can be seen to be still in water although only one chamber is gated today. The bridge in the middle ground carries Danbury Street over the canal and the Islington Tunnel entrance is just visible in the background.

29 'TUNNEL, REGENT'S CANAL'
ISLINGTON, LONDON
1835
J. & H. S. Storer
Published by Sherwood & Company

The pictures illustrate the east entrance of the Islington Tunnel, opened in 1816, and at 960 yards, the longest canal tunnel in the capital. Originally boats were pulled through by a towing boat which dragged itself through by means of a chain resting on the canal bed but this system was withdrawn in the 1930s and boats now travel through under their own power.

30 'CITY BASIN, REGENT'S CANAL'
LONDON
1828
T. H. Shepherd / E. J. Havell
Published by Jones & Company

City Road Basin was one of a number of city centre basins used for unloading incoming seaborne freight. This former industrial site fell into decline in the 1950s and 60s but has been subject to residential redevelopment and improved public access to the waterway by the London Borough of Islington. The engraving shows heavy use by commercial boats, not long after the canal had been constructed.

31 'MACCLESFIELD BRIDGE, REGENT'S PARK'
LONDON
1827

T. H. Shepherd / R. Acon
Published by Jones & Company

In the early hours of October 10 1874, the barge 'Tilbury' was being towed with other barges by a steam tug, laden with, amongst other general cargo, 5 tons of gunpowder. As the barge passed under Macclesfield Bridge, Regent's Canal, London, illustrated here, the gunpowder caught fire resulting in an enormous explosion which destroyed the bridge, killed the crew and panicked the animals in nearby London Zoo. It has since been familiarly known as 'Blow up Bridge'.

32 'GREENWICH HOSPITAL'
GT. LONDON
1800
Schnebbelic / A. Marron
'Dr. Hughson's Description of London'

The view is of the Royal Naval Hospital which became the Royal Naval College in 1873 and part of which was taken over in 1937 by the National Maritime Museum which is the leading maritime museum of the United Kingdom. This spectacular building consists of the Queen's House dating from 1635 and two separate wings joined by colonnades built between 1807 and 1816. The Museum contains models, displays, paintings and trophies, a library, and hosts lectures and special exhibitions.

33 'ISLEWORTH'
GT. LONDON
1806
Schnebblic / A. Warren
Published by I. Stratford
'Dr. Hughson's Description of London'

Dating back to the 14th century, All Saints' Church Isleworth in the centre of the engraving was largely rebuilt in 1706 by Sir Christopher Wren who incorporated the 15th century tower. In 1943 some schoolboys set fire to the church but the ancient tower survived to be built into the current 1970 brick building creating a highly individual appearance.

To the left of the church is 'The London Apprentice' a well-known Thames-side pub with a tunnel linking it to the church and believed to have been used by smugglers.

34 'TWICKENHAM, MIDDLESEX'
GT. LONDON
1814
J. P. Neale / J. Lewis
Published by John Harris
'Beauties of England and Wales'

The island on the left of the engraving is Eel Pie Island with St. Mary's Church Twickenham to its right. The church collapsed in 1713 leaving the ragstone tower to which a replacement church was rapidly rebuilt in brick creating another unusual mix of building styles. To the far right is a waterside house that probably still survives today as Ferry House and to its left, one of these buildings is now the White Swan public house which can also be seen as the white building to the far left of the photograph. Unfortunately tree growth has made the exact engraving view impossible to replicate and the church is situated about 250 yards to the left of the White Swan, hidden behind Eel Pie Island.

35 'RICHMOND'
GT. LONDON
1805
Schnebbelic / Hawkins
Published by John Harris
'Beauties of England and Wales'

Richmond Bridge which is a Grade l listed building was completed in 1777 as a five arch, stone toll bridge to replace the Richmond/East Twickenham ferry. Although widened in 1940 it remains the oldest surviving Thames bridge in London.

The magnificent building the 'Royal Star and Garter Home' for disabled ex-Service personnel established by Queen Mary and the British Red Cross in 1916 is situated on Richmond Hill and can be seen on the skyline towards the right hand side of the photograph.

36 'KINGSTON BRIDGE'
KINGSTON UPON THAMES, GT. LONDON
1839
N. Whittock / J. Rogers
Published by George Virtue

This Grade II listed, five arch, Portland stone bridge was opened by the Duke of Clarence in 1828 to replace the previous timber bridge. Although its appearance was maintained on both occasions, it was widened in 1914 and again in 2000 when it was opened by HRH the Duke of Kent in 2001.

To the right of the engraving is the tower of All Saints' Church Kingston which is famous as the place where six Saxon kings were crowned. Unfortunately it is no longer possible to include it in the same view as Richmond Bridge and it is situated off the right hand side of the photograph.

37 'THE THAMES AT COWAY STAKES'
WALTON ON THAMES, GT. LONDON
1850

Coway Stakes is an ancient ford across the River Thames near Walton on Thames. Whilst its exact location is difficult to establish today, it is generally accepted that it was situated at the bottom of the bow in the Thames west of Walton Bridge and opposite Halliford. My photograph is of this peaceful section of the Thames from the south bank to give an idea of its tranquil appearance today.

38 'SUNBURY LOCKS'
SUNBURY ON THAMES, SURREY
c.1840
Tombleson / Lacey
Published by Tombleson

Today's twin locks, the older manual one built in 1856 and its mechanised neighbour added in 1927 replace the 1812 lock which was situated a short distance upstream, next to the lock house which still survives today. To the right of the engraving can be seen St Mary's Church Sunbury which was built in 1752, restored in 1972 and is mentioned in Charles Dickens' Oliver Twist. The characteristically shaped church tower is still visible towards the left hand side of the photograph.

39 'STAINES BRIDGE'
STAINES, SURREY
1839
C. Marshall / J. Henshall

Staines Bridge, built in granite by Sir John Rennie was opened by King William IV in 1832 and is still in use today. The people in the engraving who appear to have arrived by boat are surrounding the London Stone. This stone originally marked the tidal limit of the River Thames and therefore the upstream limit of the city corporation's control of the river. A small replica stone is situated in the Lammas Pleasure Ground but the original is now in the museum attached to Staines Library.

40 'KEW BRIDGE, FROM THE FERRY
AT BRENTFORD'
KEW, LONDON
c.1790

J. Sewell
Published in the European Magazine

Beneath the arches of the 1789 granite toll bridge, opened by King George III, can be seen the timbers of the 1759 wooden bridge which had not then been demolished. Due to the weight of traffic and difficulties of access, the third and current bridge, designed by Sir John Wolfe Barry and Cuthbert Brereton was built using Cornish granite and opened by Edward VII and Queen Alexandra in 1903.

41 'BEAUMONT LODGE, NEAR OLD WINDSOR'
BERKSHIRE
1819
S. Owen / W. B. Cooke
From 'Views on the Thames' by William-Bernard Cooke and George Cooke

What an idyllic setting Beaumont Lodge occupies in the engraving, on the banks of the River Thames! This elegant building, now the White House Hotel on Burfield Road, still enjoys a rural environment within 40 acres of landscaped grounds but both Burfield Road and the busy A308 Staines to Windsor road now pass between the former Lodge and the Thames.

42 'DORNEY CHURCH, BUCKS'
BOVENEY, BUCKINGHAMSHIRE
c.1840

Tombleson / Sands
Published by Tombleson & Company

Wrongly titled Dorney Church, this church, constructed of chalk rubble and flint, has just undergone a major restoration by the Friends of Friendless Churches. It is in fact the church of St Mary Magdalene situated on a remote part of the River Thames at the hamlet of Boveney. Redundant since 1975, it had been a place of worship since before the Norman Conquest and was probably used by waterborne and riverside folk involved in transporting timber from Windsor Forest.

43 'A VIEW OF CLIEFDEN (sic) HOUSE
FROM MAIDENHEAD BRIDGE'
MAIDENHEAD, BERKSHIRE
c.1770

Cliveden is an Italianate stately home once owned by the Astors and now part of the National Trust. Set on cliffs, 200 feet above the River Thames, the present Grade I listed, Victorian, Palladian style, three-storey mansion was built in 1851, replacing the two previous houses built on the site, both destroyed by fire. The photograph was taken from the Thames Path on the opposite side of the river, from which very limited views of the house are available.

44 'HEDSOR'
BUCKINGHAMSHIRE
1840
Tombleson / W. Taylor
Published by Tombleson & Company

This beautiful view of Hedsor House from across the River Thames is not possible today due to tree growth. The 1775 house, frequently visited by King George III and Queen Charlotte was badly damaged by fire in 1795 and replaced by the current magnificent Italian Villa style stately home in 1868. It is now run as an elegant wedding and corporate event venue. The surrounding park is Grade II listed on the English Heritage National Register of Historic Parks and Gardens.

45 'HARLEYFORD HOUSE'
MARLOW, BUCKINGHAMSHIRE
1817
S. Owen / W. B. Cooke
From 'Views on the Thames' by William-Bernard Cooke and George Cooke

Harleyford Estate, now a leisure complex of marina, holiday homes, golf course and wedding venue, includes grounds attributed to the 18th century landscape designer, Capability Brown. The manor house was built in red brick in 1755 by architect Sir Robert Taylor and was the seat of Sir William Clayton, Bart.

46 'WALLINGFORD, BERKSHIRE'
1818
F.W.I. Stockdale / J. Greig

From 'Antiquarian Itinerary', published by Clarke, Murray, Bagster, Richardson and Sherwood

Wallingford, one of the oldest Royal Boroughs is a vibrant market town now in Oxfordshire. The bridge which crosses the River Thames at this point is a 900 feet long medieval stone structure. Behind it is the Georgian St. Peter's Church marked by its distinctive, slender spire and octagonal belfry. The church is no longer used for regular worship and is in the care of the Churches Conservation Trust.

47 'OSNEY LOCK'
OXFORD
1894

Osney lock, on the River Thames not far from the centre of Oxford, originated from a flash weir in the 13th century and was built in 1790 by inmates imprisoned in Oxford Castle. The lock was converted to hydraulic operation in 1970.

48 'ENTRANCE TO THE TUNNEL, LEADING TO SAPPERTON HILL, GLOUCESTERSHIRE'
THAMES AND SEVERN CANAL
1792

The Sapperton Tunnel, after 5 years in the digging, was opened in 1789 and at 3817 yards is the longest broadbeam tunnel in the country. It is situated in the middle of the Thames and Severn Canal which led from Lechlade on the River Thames in the east to Saul Junction on the Gloucester and Sharpness Canal in the west. Sadly, after the last loaded boat passed over the summit in 1911, parts of the canal were gradually abandoned and the tunnel itself is currently blocked by a roof collapse. Restoration is the ambition of the Cotswolds Canals Trust which operates boat trips into the tunnel. The Coates Portal at the eastern end which appears in this picture, was rebuilt in 1976/7. The Tunnel House Inn on the top of the hill to the left was rebuilt following a fire in 1952 and is still open today.

49 'AQUEDUCT OF THE KENNET AND AVON CANAL
AT LIMPLEY STOKE, NEAR BATH'
WILTSHIRE
1864

This classical, Bath stone aqueduct is known as Dundas Aqueduct, named in honour of Charles Dundas, the first chairman of the Kennet and Avon Canal Company. Situated near the village of Limpley Stoke, 4 miles south east of Bath on the A36, it is 137 metres long with three arches and carries the Kennet and Avon Canal over the River Avon and the Wessex Main Line railway from Bath to Westbury which can be seen in the foreground of the photograph. Built by John Rennie and completed in 1805, the aqueduct developed leaks and was closed from 1954 until 1984 when it was reopened following extensive polythene and concrete relining work.

50 'THE OLD BRIDGE, BATH'
1829
T. H. Shepherd / J. B. Allen

It is hard to believe that this fine, five arch stone bridge, built in 1754 to carry the Bristol Road over the River Avon to the South Gate of the beautiful city of Bath could have been replaced in 1964 by what is little more than a slab of reinforced concrete. Known as Churchill Bridge it deservedly lurks in shame low above the water level of the River Avon running just below.